C. Markell Davis-Haynes

THE 23RD PSALM

UNDERSTANDING THE BENEFITS OF MAKING THE LORD YOUR SHEPHERD

ME
WE

MORE EXCELLENT
WAY ENTERPRISES

Publisher:
MEWE, LLC
Lithonia, GA
www.mewellc.com

First Edition
ISBN: 978-0-692-53939-2

For Worldwide Distribution

*To my supportive husband, Chevaughn M. Haynes,
for the many years of happiness and exciting
memories and for being my biggest fan.*

*To my awesome brothers, Mark and Chris Davis for
standing beside me in ministry and encouraging me to
be all that God has called me to be.*

*To the BEST CHURCH on the planet,
Anointed Word Christian Ministries International in
Ellenwood, Georgia, thank you for being awesome.
Thanks for attending church faithfully and listening to
me preach/teach weekly. Most importantly, thank you
for applying the messages to your daily lives.*

*In Loving Memory of my parents Michael and Carol
Davis. You guys were the best role models ever! Your
leadership and parenting skills still speaks clearly to
me. I pray that I have made you proud.
Forever in my heart.
Let's all continue to make God's name great!*

I love you all.

*"**The 23rd Psalm** by Apostle Markell Haynes is a cutting edge must read! Her sensitivity and awareness of the Holy Spirit from her early experiences as a child to adulthood, will evoke a wellspring of revelation. Her Upbringing in Holiness has prepared her on the back side of the mountain to be revealed in this season."*

Rev. Dr. Collette L. Gunby, Senior Pastor
Green Pastures Christian Ministries

*"**The 23rd Psalm** by Apostle Haynes is a must read book for any believer who desires to walk in a closer relationship with God – trusting Him in every situation that emanates from their daily walk. I found this book to be a refreshing look at this much beloved chapter of Psalms. Read it for yourself and then share it with another believer who is striving to walk in victory."*

Bishop Ruth Smith Holmes, Senior Pastor
Light of the World Christian Ministries

"The 23rd Psalm is a passage of scripture that all of us learned as a child. Many will read this psalm strictly devotionally or when seeking solace and comfort in times of trouble. Ms. Davis-Haynes effectively exposits this very familiar psalm and leads the reader to a deeper understanding of God's desires and promises toward the believer. From her discussion of the necessity of one's submission to God as Lord as the foundation to a fuller understanding of the promises of God in the passage, Ms. Davis-Haynes takes the reader on an enriching journey through the abundant life believers can expect."

Dr. Donnie Peal, Executive Director
ORU Educational Fellowship

"This book gives such inspirational insights on the Lord being our Shepherd, leading and guiding us through the tough times when we don't see or understand how we are going to get from here to there. Pastor Markell's goal is to encourage us to use our time in prayer and supplications as we trust God in all facets of life. We think this book leads us right into God's arms of protections without fear."

Apostle Dallas & Pastor Janet Ellis
United Full Gospel Revival Center Ministries

"Thanks to this message, the 23rd Psalm has become my life. I have learned that if you truly make God the LORD over everything in your life, then all the blessings of life become yours. This message taught me those blessings and knowing them has made me declare again: THE LORD IS MY SHEPERD! After reading this book, I challenge you to declare: THE LORD IS YOUR SHEPERD and watch what HE can truly do."

Elder Christopher Davis
Anointed Word Christian Ministries International

"Praise God forever! Apostle Haynes has, by the grace of God, taken one of the gold standards of the Bible, the 23rd Psalm, and given us a book that will permeate ones heart and soul. Apostle Haynes meticulously takes the wisdom of her parents and teachers, and articulates to readers, young and old, a practical and relatable journey of making God the LORD and Shepherd of all that pertains to our total lives."

Bishop W. Michael Leach
Flames of Fire Ministries International, Inc.

"Fresh, easy to read, personal, and well-written with a message much more than surface deep! Apostle Haynes probes, challenge and encourages us to reappraise, reexamine ourselves, and to live day by day acknowledging that God is truly The LORD my Shepherd and not "co-" in any sense of the matter or any area of our lives ...therefore, 'I shall not want!'"

Prophetess Gwen Leach, Senior Pastor
Flames of Fire Ministries International, Inc.

TABLE OF CONTENTS

ACKNOWLEDGEMENTS

To the dynamic pastors who have poured into my life over the years.

To Min. C. Dudley and MEWE Publishing and Mr. Marcus Shepard and the graphic designers of SharperFX, thank you for making my book an eye seeing reality.

FOREWORD

How many times have you been asked to recite the 23rd Psalm and you sigh in the back of your mind? How many times have you blah-blah-blah-ed over the words because you didn't know the prayer or you mumbled over it because you didn't feel like saying it? Or when you hear the preacher say, "Turn your Bibles to Psalms 23," do your eyes roll to the back of your head?

I was at church when Pastor Markell started her series and she said, "Turn your Bibles to Psalms 23." My eyes started rolling and I sighed (in my mind), and I was like, "She's preaching the 23rd Psalms again? How many times can preachers talk about the same scripture?" Yes, I must admit it was all me. My flesh was so used to hearing the song, hearing people recite it, and just reading it myself.

Before hearing her message, the 23rd Psalm had become rhetoric. It had become the prayer you said before the football game, or the prayer you would say so you wouldn't offend anyone.

However, when this young awesome woman of GOD started reading the word of GOD, she started TEACHING the word of GOD. I was floored from what Pastor was saying and how she broke it down to it couldn't be broken down no more!

This book will transform your life! The analogies, the examples, and the stories are all apart of how you will be able to take her words, parallel them to GOD'S words, apply them to your life, and experience change.

As the oldest, I respect, I applaud, I esteem, and I honor my baby sister. She is named after our brother, Christopher, and I (Mark). Daddy told us her name, and that she had been named after the both of us. But when Momma started to call her Chrislyn, I asked, "Where is my baby?"

If I had to have a Christian role model… she would be the one! Not because she totes a Bible around all day long or that she is a Holy Roller; but because her beautiful smile heals broken hearts, her words encourage new life, and her very presence brings about change. I've seen the LORD prepare a table before her in the presence of her enemy.

My hat goes off to you. Momma and Daddy, Chris, and I are so very proud of you. For the last 35 years, I have enjoyed watching "MY BABY" grow up to now being "MY BIG SISTA" and "MY PASTOR". I love seeing GOD working through and in your life and how you have affected the life of others in the church, in the school, and in our community. I pray GOD's favor and HIS blessings over your life and I pray that GOODNESS and MERCY follow you all the days of your life. I LOVE YOU.

Bishop Mark Maxey Davis
Anointed Word Christian Ministries International, Inc.
Anointed Word Christian Schools International, Inc.

GO EAGLES!!!

For as long as I can remember, I have been able to quote the 23rd Psalm almost as well as I can recite the alphabet. This passage of scripture has been ingrained in many believers since childhood; however, oftentimes, we fail to truly understand the real meaning of the Lord as our Shepherd. This book does not merely depict a casual relationship with the Shepherd, it is a testimony of a relationship forged and developed over many years of an intimate relationship with a Shepherd who truly watches over and cares for his flock.

The 23rd Psalm: Understanding the Benefits of Making the Lord Your Shepherd is an appropriate book for the times. It serves as an instructional manual for Godly living. This book is personal and insightful, yet spirit provoking and inspiring. A book written from a heart that has experienced the love of God and a heart that has allowed God to rule, to guide and to reign in her life. Life is a journey, but the author so eloquently guides the reader down a path that makes the navigation of life successful. *The 23rd Psalm* eliminates all fear and releases confidence and peace in every area of life.

This amazing work should be a part of every believer's library. Young Christians will receive instructions as they grow in their relationship with God and mature saints will be reinforced and revived. The reader will truly understand the importance of getting to know the Lord as a Shepherd. Love you.

Pastor Maurice Dukes
Cornerstone of Faith Christian Church

PREFACE

As a child, were you forced to learn the 23rd Psalm by your parents or youth ministry leader? Did your parents or grandparents constantly make you recite, memorize or read it from the Bible over and over again?

Even though you memorized it, recited it, or read it repeatedly, did you fully understand the real meaning of this precious and most reverenced chapter in the Holy Bible? Well, this book, *The 23rd Psalm*, will help you to have a greater understanding of this passage of scripture so that you will be able to apply the spiritual and practical concepts to your life for victorious living.

My prayer is that you move from just knowing this very life-changing chapter of Psalms – that you may have learned as a child – to actually relating to it and experiencing its benefits as an adult. God's promises are expressed throughout the verses of Psalm 23 and as a believer, who is aware of and fully understand those promises, you are able to trust God to provide your every need.

From the Lord being your Shepherd to your dwelling in the house of the Lord forever, prepare to receive spiritual revelation as you walk in the divine guidance of the Almighty God.

CHAPTER 1

The LORD
Guides and Rescues Me

"The LORD is my shepherd; I shall not want."
(Psalm 23:1)

On a particular Sunday, while I was preparing a sermon, the LORD told me to remind His people of the importance of the 23rd chapter of the book of Psalms. He wanted them to have a clear insight into the quintessence of divine guidance on a day-to-day basis in their lives.

Coincidentally, on that fulgent morning during a prayer session, an intercessor started praying and thanking the Almighty God for being His Shepherd. He was already operating in the realm of the message I had prepared. What a confirmation of God's word to me! From this, I could see that God had something major He wanted to do in our lives that Sunday morning.

For easy understanding of the Bible passage, it's good to do justice to the verses one after the other. Now, let us begin with the first verse of the 23rd chapter of the book of Psalms. This song depicts a personal encounter with God—between one individual and the Almighty God. When reading it, you have to take into perspective the fact that it is talking about you, your relationship and your encounter with God.

I can boldly tell you that the LORD is my Shepherd, but my testimony will effect nothing in your life because you might not have experienced the LORD as being your Shepherd. I can only tell you about Him, but I can't directly transmit my personal encounter to you as experiential knowledge.

You too must *know* Him personally - it's all about you and God. That's the first key you should note.

Allow GOD to be the LORD of Your Life

The reason most of us do not always experience the supernatural levels of God—walking in the valley of the shadow of death up to the level where God prepares a table before us in the presence of our enemies—is mainly because we have not allowed God to be the LORD over our lives. In this chapter, the keyword we will be looking at is *LORD*.

A lot of importance has been put on the word *Shepherd,* but in reality, the actual emphasis should be on the name LORD. Why? It is because you need to make a specific distinction as to who is leading you when you refer to God as LORD, even though you're giving Him total control. We need to understand that there are many shepherds. For instance, we have 20 Shepherds in my local church. Are they my Shepherds? Of course not. In the same vein, there are many lords. Sarah referred to Abraham her husband as her lord. Was he really the lord over her? Therefore, the principal thing we have to do is to identify the person who is leading us. And in this scripture, the emphasis is on a person, *the Lord.* Some versions of the Bible even capitalize all the letters of the name LORD.

It was about two years ago, when I taught about the difference between LORD and Lord. LORD gives distinct recognition to God the Father. Lord may be a leader in the church or your boss. In Biblical times and even now, you may have Lords and slaves. When people address a nobleman, they say, "My Lord." It's a way of showing honor and respect for the status you accord a particular person in your life. For example, the children at our school call me Mrs. Haynes. They place 'Mrs.' in front of my name to show a specific position of respect. Lord could be used for people who are in leadership, have people under them as their subordinates, or have some kind of power.

However, it is important to distinguish the kind of Lord we were talking about here. David, the young shepherd, God's prototype who was courageous and strong in war - the child giant-slayer, and the writer of Psalm 23, had to use capital letters in LORD so that we would not get this confused. He wanted readers to know that the LORD God is his Shepherd.

The Role of the Shepherd

What is the responsibility of a shepherd? It is to watch over, lead, keep and protect the sheep. From what? Wolves. Here, David understood how to compare God to an actual shepherd because he himself was one. He understood and carried out his duty in caring for the sheep. David dare not come back home from the field to tell his father that he lost five sheep because a lion, a tiger, or a bear invaded where they were to take the animals away. The sheep were livestock and they had value because they were animals that people usually sacrificed unto the LORD in those days. David also understood that his role as a shepherd was important. Even though some might have said, "Oh, what has he done? He's just out there looking after a flock of sheep," but yes, he took care of those little sheep because he had an important role in their lives - he must always watch over them so as protect them against the onslaught of invaders and robbers. David's total dedication to his role made him very powerful as a leader.

David could fight, battle against and even kill lions, bears, and wolves with his bare hands; he was there to keep those dangerous beasts from hurting or killing the sheep. So, when he began to look closely at the personality of God as LORD, he realized that there were similarities between God and himself. He knew that God was responsible for making sure that things are in good order in his own life, just as he was responsible for the lives of the sheep. The sheep needed protection and leadership. They are generally known to be ignorant, and many consider them to be one of the stupid animals on earth. That's why they needed a shepherd to tell them, "Come back, sweetie. You aren't doing this right. Come on, honey. No, no, no."

In this way, David began to realize that God was looking out for his best interests in the same way he cared for the best interests of his father's sheep.

In his lifetime, David found himself in and out of trouble. He was always doing something he wasn't supposed to be doing. He was constantly found in sinful situations, for which he had to repent. He killed Uriah in order to cover up the adultery he committed with his wife. But then, did God give David the permission to keep on sinning because his heart was pure toward God and that he always had a repentant heart? No. God considered David to be his friend. Inasmuch as he always understood his misdeeds, he never thought it twice before he would make things right with God. Now, before you can even go on with the rest of the 23rd chapter of the book of Psalms, you have to ascertain whether God is the LORD of your life or you have simply made Him a lord like most people do in today's world.

Your job, your marriage, your husband, your wife, and even *you* can be considered your lord. In other words, if care is not taken, you would put them in the first place in your life while God would be relegated to the second place. When this occurs, you try to use God as a back-up as you attempt to be your own lord. Instead of saying, "God, I give you full and complete control over my life," you'll begin to say, "I just need you to help me as I make decisions in my life." Sometimes, we find ourselves doing this and we don't even realize that we've done just that.

Jesus Is Not Your Co-Pilot

There used to be an old saying, "Jesus is my co-pilot." The saying should actually be, "Jesus is my pilot." If I were to say that Jesus is my co-pilot, then I'm making myself equal to Him. If two people work at the same company and they are in the same position, neither is greater than the other. They are co-workers. You don't call your boss your co-worker. Why? This is because your boss has the authority to guide you on the job by acting as a shepherd and also as a lord.

If I also say that Jesus is my co-pilot or God is my co-pilot, then I'm saying that God and I have the same abilities—the same authority—and as long as we are working together, we're going to get where we are supposed to be. Well, in actual sense, that's not the way it's supposed to be, but a lot of people say it because it sounds so deep. If anything at all, you should be saying, "Jesus, you're my LORD. Take the wheel, lead me, and I shall follow." My brother told me once that Jesus needs to be the wheel and not just take the wheel. When you begin to realize you are not on the same level as God, you'll begin to walk in a place of submission to His sovereignty. You will no longer struggle with Him in making life's choices and decisions. We have to believe that God is LORD, which means that He is the Supreme Person in every aspect of our lives. Therefore, we have to submit to however He chooses to govern our lives. When you make someone your LORD, you will submit to His established rules and authority.

God doesn't approve man's plan; He only commends a person who always lives in subjection to His plan whether it's convenient or not. Being that person means that you've made Him the LORD over your life without any reservation. If He is your LORD and He calls, you'll say, "Yes, LORD," asking no questions. There won't be any argument with Him on anything. Remember, sheep depend on the direction and wisdom of the shepherd. You'll want to leave *everything* in His hands.

Again, we have to make sure that we understand this one word, LORD, and also make sure we fully comprehend the terms and agreements that come along with it. In other words, we've got to understand the terms and conditions that come with making God our LORD. Today, it's quite unfortunate that many believers have Jesus as their Savior, but they are yet to hand over their lives to Him as their LORD and Shepherd.

When you take on a job or work for a company, you'll receive a manual that states all the terms and conditions that come with taking the job – all of the responsibilities and requirements associated with your new position would be clearly stated. Now, somewhere in fine print, there may be words that say, "And other responsibilities that may be related to, but not listed." When you are aware of the salary and other employment benefits that are associated with the job, you'll be able to make a decision right at that moment whether or not you are willing to submit to the terms and conditions. As a result, you can decide if it is the right job. It's the same way we have to be with God. When we begin to look unto God as our complete LORD, we have to understand that we cannot continue to do what we did in the past. We cannot make decisions without consulting with Him.

If God chooses to take a particular thing away from me, I have to be content with it. If He chooses to make me go through something, I have to go along with

His plan. This is because allowing Him to lead me is part of the terms and conditions that come with making Him my LORD. When we agree to make God our LORD, there are good and bad things that we will experience in our lives. Submission to God's leadership comes with definite consequences and perks, including some *hard* things or tough times that we must endure without any complaint. Allowing God to guide us requires us to submit our flesh to His spirit. We may not fully understand what God is doing, but we have to be in full agreement because the good outweighs the bad, and there are benefits to enjoy from this divine relationship when it's time for us to "retire." I am confident that I can go with the package that God has presented. I will let Him have complete control. I will allow Him to be my leader, my God, my Shepherd.

Learn to be Content

As long as you agree to allow God to be your Shepherd, there is nothing else you are going to need. Just say to yourself, "I shall not want." Once you have read and accepted all of the terms and conditions that come with making God your LORD, make up your mind to be content with what He gives you. Yes, make sure you have contentment. Both in plenty and in want, learn to be content. This is the way the LORD works. He will not give you things He knows you're not capable of handling.

Let's consider a case study. Tamara and Ashton are parents, and they have three children, but they treat the kids differently. The way they converse with one child is different from that of others. Because of the differences in the children's personalities, their parents usually relate with them individually as follows:

> Tabatha is very sensitive. If you say something out of place, she would retort, saying, "That's not nice." Because of her sensitive nature, it would be fruitless for her parents to start shout on her whenever she reacts that way. You can look at her and she will straighten up.

> Now, Summer is a different person in the sense that you may have to do more than just look at her before she will straighten up.

> Then there is Ashley. She has just become a teenager and feels like she knows everything. Her parents constantly have to threaten her with punishment because of her unruly attitude. She always wants to be independent in her own world where she would no longer be subject to parental guidance. Therefore, experience becomes her best teacher.

Likewise, God does not deal with all of us in the same way. He may decide to give one sheep a $50,000 a year job, another sheep a $200,000 a year job, and give yet another sheep a $20,000 per year job. This does not mean He likes one sheep more than the other. Besides, God always puts our individual weaknesses and strengths into consideration in His dealings with us.

Remember the parable of servants who received different amount of talents from their master, even according to their abilities.

God wants us to learn the importance of contentment in whatever state we find ourselves. The person receiving the $20,000 a year job may be prone to splurge, and so if God gives him $200,000 dollars a year, he will splurge it and has nothing to show for his income. Then, it would look like the LORD Himself has set him up for failure. In another instance, the person making $200,000 per year may be getting the big head because of his earnings. He looks at the person making $20,000 and wants to make a mockery. It is the same God who is the provider for the person making $200,000 as well as the person making $20,000 a year – God is still the Shepherd and LORD over both of them.

When God is leading you and you have things going on in your life that you don't understand, you just have to say, "LORD, I'm trusting you anyway." That's the valley of the shadow of death. When I'm making an income and it still seems like it's not enough to cover the bills, that's the valley, but even in that, I will not fear. Why? The simple truth is that God is with me; my Shepherd is with me. I have come to the place of trusting God every day of my life, and it works well for me. In the past, my question was, "Well, God, why do you bless one person this way and another person that way? Why is this person prosperous in this area, but I feel like I'm still struggling in the same thing?" I have come to the place of trusting God and accepting the terms and conditions that come with making the LORD my Shepherd. So I have to be at rest in my mind that whatever comes my way, God has taught me to say, "It is well." It may be hard, but all the same, it is well.

Are you financially weak or handicapped? Remember, if a shepherd finds out that one sheep is weak among his flock, he wouldn't drive it hard, or shout on it, "Get up, poor sheep! Why can't you walk? Don't delay us!" No. He would carry the sheep on His shoulders and give it a special attention and care, knowing full well that the sheep is in the valley. That's what God does for His children. He knows how to take care of you in your financial downtime. Yes, you may not have up to $200,000 dollars in the bank, but your house rent is paid on time, even though you only make $20,000 a year. I want you to see the LORD as your Shepherd. You may not ever make $200,000 a year, but your cupboards are always filled with good things. You may have many kids, but they are all clothed, bathed, fed, and smart. You may not be driving a Cadillac, but a 1995 Dodge. Guess what? You're moving forward in your life. Wherever I find myself, I've learned to be content because the LORD is my Shepherd. He understands what's good for me at every moment of my life. Trust the LORD alone. You will miss God looking at other people.

You will miss your wants being taken care of by looking at another person for help that *only* God can give. In the Scriptures, David professed, saying, "I shall not want," rather than "I shall not need." Although there is a world of difference between needs and wants, the

Shepherd has promised to provide for the two. The scripture in question lets me know that God does not only provide my needs, but also grant my heart's desires – I shall not want. Now, if I am too busy looking at how God is my neighbor's Shepherd and not my own Shepherd, I'm going to miss everything that He has for me. I am still going to be in want and I will never become satisfied with God.

Many people are missing God today, yet they walk around, saying, "He's my Shepherd, He's my LORD." That's an oxymoron. They don't really have experiential knowledge of the role of the LORD as the Shepherd. Why serve a God who does not satisfy you? Why serve a God who does not give you what you want. Although our parents taught us Psalms 23, we never really fully understood that we were committing ourselves to the LORD. When you have $200,000, you have $200,000 worth of problems and bills. It is the same with a person who earns $20,000 a year, he or she will have problematic issues as well, though they may not come in a great magnitude that often goes along with making a substantial amount of money. I want you to understand that there is nothing that you'll lack when you've understood where God is in your life as your Shepherd.

Trust God in Your Marriage

Ideally, I cannot make my marriage a standard to judge another person's marriage. If you are married, your desires in your marriage may be different from mine.

Together with my spouse, I've allowed God to be the LORD over my marriage, and I've chosen to be content always. Am I going to accept foolishness? No. Are we going to treat each other like dogs? No. If that's what you want in your marriage, well, that's you. It is not what I want in a marriage. I know some people who get married for business deals. It's a partnership. One would say to the other, "I'm in debt, and you have a better income, so let's make this thing happen. I put my name on something and you put your name on something, we could both blow up." It's a business transaction, and then when it falls apart, you have nothing because you did not allow the LORD to be the Shepherd over your marriage.

In our marriage relationship, we may pass through the valley of the shadow of death. What is the valley in the marriage? Health issues can be a valley. All of a sudden, your spouse could be stricken with cancer and you have to figure out how you are going to take care of loved one. If your spouse loses his/her job, how would you cope when your family is used to living on two sources of income? Perhaps, you have a *blended* family now, because you are married to somebody who has children from a previous marriage, and the kids are raising hell, what would you do? These are valley experiences. If our children have gone crazy in regard to their behavior and now we have to figure out a way to bring them back in, then, that's a valley.

Another example is when one spouse goes out and buys something and the other spouse knows nothing about the decision, and somehow everything turns upside down such that the bank account is out of balance. That's a valley. However, if we honestly make the LORD the Shepherd over our marriage, even through the valley, He is there with us, and we will eventually come out victorious. Just like the children of Israel came out of the wilderness after 40 years, we will eventually come out if we make a decision to trust God wholeheartedly.

Generally speaking, allow the LORD to be the LORD over every sphere of your life and learn how to respect His role therein. Ask Him to help you become content with the role you play in being the sheep. Reading the rest of Psalms 23 will be null and void if you are not content with your role in this divine relationship that joins two persons - the Shepherd and the sheep...that is *you*.

Spend Time with the Shepherd

To truly know the extent of how great the Almighty God can be LORD in your life requires that you spend quality time with Him. When you become a Christian, everything about God becomes accessible to you. Just like my cell phone comes with many apps, God comes into my life with many things that can be maximized to make my life better. In His divine apps, you would find Him good enough to be the following – provider, healer, refuge, strong tower, present help, shepherd, deliverer, friend, brother, and the list goes on.

God is everything to us and He works with us to accomplish everything. We have to utilize all of the apps that God makes available to us. The Bible says He has *"blessed us with all spiritual blessings in heavenly places in Christ Jesus."* (Ephesians 1:3) God has not withheld anything from you. So, for instance, don't say, "Right now, I only need a message," and just go to stick on prophetic app without checking out other apps. What do you think would happen if you do that? You'll never get the fullness of the benefits you have, right at your fingertips. Why on earth should you opt for anything less than all He has provided? Why did you surrender your life to the LORD in the first place if you only want few of His blessings? You may have seen Him in the lives of others and desired Him too, then go for His highest deal.

Just like you use all of the apps on your phone to make full utilization of the mobile device, you have to use all of the benefits that God has made available to you. Of course, the outside appearance of the phone is one thing, but learning how to perform tasks to make your daily activities easier is something else. It's quite funny that there are many people with expensive phones, who don't know how to do anything more than make a call or send a message on the device. Honey, there is so much more to a smartphone! You need to pull out the manual and learn how to do more; investigate the different apps and use them so that having the phone can enhance your life greatly. For instance, if you hit the app for maps and type in where you want to go, will it literally lead you? God will also lead you; not only will He lead you, but HE will also give you the destination. How amazing is that!

God says, "*In all thy ways acknowledge me and I will direct your path.*" (Proverbs 3:6) Moreover, if I briefly look at the directions and then put my phone down, I will still be lost except I review and follow the instructions completely. It is the same way in our relationship with God. We have to allow God to guide us completely. In the past, when bad things happen, it's just like scrolling through the pictures in the phone. You have to say, "Okay LORD, I trust you with this sensitive area in my life. How can I erase it? How can I get myself to a point where my mind as well as my life is not stagnated? God is telling you that there are some pictures that need to be placed in the 'trash' of your phone, and you say, "Well, God, if I put them in the trash, I won't be able to see them again." So, you decide to save it on your SIM card and then hit delete. Not following God's instructions is like you're trying to be the co-pilot in such area of your life. As a result, ten years later, you thought you had dealt with something, but it's still there, because it is still in your SIM card. Well, God has ordered you to trash it; you have to be ready to obey Him.

Now, I want you to consider the work of a phone assistant called *Siri* that can talk back to you when you make an inquiry on a matter. When you ask her a question, she will provide an answer. For example, you may ask her, "How do I get over alcoholism?" When Siri responds, you only need to follow the information provided. Well, when God starts talking, when He wants to respond to our questions, He may send somebody to help you with your situation. Instead of disagreeing with

God and replying, "Man, that's not what I need. That's a bunch of crap. If I do that, I'll be back where I was and become even worse," you need to follow the instructions. When you walk in disobedience, you have limited His abilities to be LORD in your life, and this means He's no longer allowed to be the good Shepherd in your life. Don't miss out on your blessings just because you don't want to fulfill your part in that contract, which He requires you to do. The Bible says, *"The spirit is indeed willing, but the flesh is weak."* (Matthew 26:41) When you're making God the LORD and Shepherd of your life, there will always be a battle between the flesh and the spirit. Why? The devil does not want the flesh to be under the control of the spirit, HE knows that if that happens, HE will have no say in whatsoever takes place in your life. You have to get to a point in your life when you'll say, "Whether good or bad, God is my LORD. My God is the Shepherd of my life."

Make Him LORD of Every Area

We have to even go beyond just paying our tithes and come to the point where we are willing to give what God tells us to give. God has shown us countless times that it is beneficial to be obedient as far as *giving* is concerned. Sometime ago, in my local church, we were going through financial hardships. God said we should give $500 to a certain ministry quickly. He also said, "You might want to have it in by the end of the week." It is quite a surprise that we have to give out money when we're trying to make money. What sense does that make? But, because I am determined to make God the

LORD of my life, I'm going to take a walk on the wild side. Even though, I may not understand the intent of the Good Shepherd right now, I am just going to give out my money. The following week, after the money had been given out, two new children joined our school, and the church's offering sky-rocketed. If I had sat there and debated the LORD's order, trying to understand why I had to give out $500 dollars, I would have missed such a blessing. If I say I'm going to trust God, then I'm going to do it because afterwards, there comes peace and blessings as rewards for my obedience. I didn't argue with Him because I had read the fine print. I had signed the contract of making Him my LORD.

I encourage you to reappraise and reexamine every aspect of your life so as to ascertain the definition of 'lord' that the Almighty God falls into in your life. Is He Lord or is He LORD, your Shepherd? In your prayer life, He may be the LORD, but in your marriage and finances He might just be the co-pilot. Even with your health, do you accept Him as your Healer, or you just say, "I know He's a healer, but I'm going to take these pills like my doctor told me. And, I'm going to be all right." We have to put our faith in all of God, and none of self.

When I was a teenager, my doctor told me that my thyroids were off, and that because of this, my weight would oscillate in measure, going up and down in an irregular manner. However, I made a decision that I would always fix my mind on the report of the LORD, my Shepherd, rather than that of the doctor. The doctor also prescribed that I should always wear a *guarder* on the side of my neck; and he also tried to put me on medication. Well, I am thankful to report that I did not have to wear the neck guarder. When my husband later asked me to marry him, I told him that he would have to marry both of us – me and the guarder. The thing did not even bug him. We eventually got married; and through it all, we prayed and God healed me. As if that was not enough, doctors said if I got pregnant, I would have a bad time in such a condition. I said within me, "Did they really think I was going to walk around with a baby inside of me, two necks, and a husband?" I had to put it all back into perspective and trust my LORD. After all, I was already doing as much as I knew with my body.

I needed a healing. I desired to be made whole. I needed a miracle. I didn't want to keep revisiting this one issue in my life. I knew that if I have accepted the LORD as the Lord over my health, something has to be sacrificed. At some point in my life, I realized that I have to be content with the fact that God knew what was best for my body. Even up till today, if He tells me to stop doing or eating something, then I have to respect whatever He says. Whether I heard it through my doctor, or found it out through research, I have to respect it; or else I'll have to face the consequences. Disobeying the LORD usually has grave consequences. Not allowing the Good Shepherd to guide me has consequences. And, there is no one you can blame when you begin to face such consequences, except yourself.

I strongly believe that if I've signed a contract and I don't hold up my end of the contract, then people may decide to come after me. God is a just God, but He is not a God who can be bribed to ignore justice in any matter. If God has sealed a deal with you, He expects you to keep to it faithfully. He is not a God who is going to take care of somebody who doesn't want Him. If you say that you don't need Him, you've simply shown that you'll be fine without Him. If you feel you can make it without Him, oh fine! It's left to you. Remember, He has given man the power of volition - we have the ability (free will) to make choices and to reason on our own with no external compulsion. So, whatever may be our reasons for not trusting God for who He is, the LORD and Shepherd, everything is up to us. But, please understand that you have to accept whatever result you get if you choose not to make the LORD over your life in any situation.

As a parent, if you make no meaningful attempt to go to church with your children, pray with them regularly, and as well train them up in the way they should go, you would find out that, if our kids are left to themselves, they have a greater chance of getting off track in the journey of their lives. Go back and reappraise your parental responsibilities and how it has so far affected the life of your children. Really, our kids may not like some of the decisions we make as parents, but then it is our job to raise them up in the way of God. My mother once told me, saying, "I don't have a whole lot of money to give you, but I gave you God. You have to get to heaven on your own. You're old enough to know if you're going to make it to heaven or not."

In every aspect of our lives, we must make sure that God is God - that He is our LORD and Shepherd. Because the LORD is our Shepherd, we shall not want. We have to allow Him to rule and reign over every aspect of our lives because He knows the best for our lives. With sincerity of heart and with our mouth, we have to confess our allegiance unto Him by declaring that He is our Shepherd. Because we have chosen God to be our LORD, we have personal convictions that we will not want for anything. It is not God who said we shall not want. We make a decision that we shall not want because He is our Shepherd, according to Psalm 23:1 that says, *"Because the LORD is my shepherd, I shall not want."* It's a big difference!

CHAPTER 2

The LORD
Gives Me Rest & Life

"He maketh me to lie down in green pastures: He leadeth me beside the still waters." (Psalm 23:2)

Unarguably, Psalm 23 is an indication that David had already made up his mind to make the LORD his Shepherd under all circumstances. Before reaching that conclusion, he had examined all of the possibilities and the benefits of accepting the LORD as the one and only head of his life. In his heart, he made an agreement with God by declaring his allegiance and making an irrevocable covenant with Him. David understood that if he made God the Shepherd of his life, God would provide everything he needed to become fulfilled in life and destiny. After all, it was God who made him and defined the destiny he had, and only God could sustain him to fulfill it. As a result, David said categorically, "I shall not want."

Declare that You Shall Not Want

What a great conviction! God did not say "I shall not want," neither did He personally tell David that he will not want for anything. These are the sayings of David himself, who believed that his wants will be met. Why? He knew that whatever the Almighty God chose to do in his life would make him feel pleased, happy and satisfied. After all, David had made God the head over his own life. As Christians, we too have to get to a point where we can say, "Okay God, I surrender my life to you and I am content with whatever you choose to do with me and my life." How many of us are willing to attain that level of abandonment of self to God and His will for our lives?

If we don't have the understanding that David had, then we are far behind in enjoying the whole package of divine providence that God has for us. Psalms 23:2 says, *"He*

maketh me to lie down in green pastures..." The amazing
thing about green pastures is that it is a place of rest,
prosperity, and good health. Since we do not look for a dirty
place when we picnic in the park; the same applies to life.

Allow the Shepherd to Order Your Steps

The LORD gives us benefits as we make Him our
Shepherd. Let's look again at Psalm 23:2, *"He maketh me..."*
He orders me, He requires me, He sets me up at the place
where I have to lie down in green pastures. Yes, the place of
God's presence and providence is characterized by
tranquility, bringing satisfaction to the soul. The word *green*
in this Bible text is a glorious keyword to note. When
something is green, it is fresh, being full of life and vitality.
Other pastures may be brown, yellowish, and drying up;
God's own pastures are forever green such that you will
always find rest in the midst of this world's turmoil.

In addition, God is saying to you, "I am with you, I
am leading you, and I am taking you through." What are those
issues in your life that are not allowing you to lie down in
green pastures? What are those situations that is going on in
your life and is keeping you from allowing God to hand you
the ability to lie down in green pastures? What is blocking
you from enjoying the peace that God gives to those He
shepherds? Take a clue from David's conviction. God is
irrevocably committed to helping you all the way. Why
should it be so hard to give yourself to Him?

> *Be careful for nothing; but in every thing by*
> *prayer and supplication with thanksgiving*
> *let your requests be made known to God.*

And the peace of God, which surpasseth all understanding shall keep your hearts and minds through Christ Jesus. (Colossians 4:6-7)

Until we make God LORD over every aspect of our lives, we won't be able to lie down in green pastures, especially in the areas where we are trying to control ourselves. We need to make God the LORD of our health so that HE can shepherd our health and cause us to be in good health all the days of our lives. In the same manner, we should make Him the God and Shepherd over our finances. It is not good for us to have a situation where our finances are a terrible mess. It is good for us to be in a position where we have a time to rest, where all the bills are paid on time, and where we have a little extra so as to save more money and do some other needful things. We have to ask ourselves if we have really made God the Shepherd of our finances.

If not so, you have to go back, reevaluate your life and ask yourself — what areas of my life are not allowing me to lie down in green pastures? If you are not prosperous in that area of your life, it may be a spiritual issue such that you are yet to declare God as your LORD; and maybe, you don't take time to read the Scriptures, you don't take time to pray, you don't give tithes, you practically do nothing and you begin to wonder, *Why do I never feel that peace in my spirit?*

There Is Life in the Shepherd

Verse two of the Psalm goes on to say, *"He leadeth me beside the still waters."* What are still waters? Calm waters, peaceful waters. Where can you naturally find still waters? Still waters can be portrayed as the beautiful, pure, and giver of life. There's a difference between God-made still water and man-made still water. Man-made water like puddles, lakes, and swamps are lifeless and dirty. However, in God-made still waters like rivers, waterfalls, streams, and the ocean, there is movement and life. Jesus is the living water, and God leads us beside the still waters to help us get refreshed as we journey in life. It's the clean, alkaline water that purifies our body.

It's essential that the LORD purifies those that He shepherds — a good detoxification process is necessary to keep our bodies clean. The water is fresh, reenergizing, and rejuvenating. Many a time, we go through some hard situations and God makes us lie down and take a break. Sometimes we pour out ourselves and exert so much pressure on our lives that God wants us to be replenished. During this process, we will be exposed to areas of our lives we need to work on; and as a result, God will begin to restore our soul. We can't be effective men and women of God, if we are a worn-out mess. It is hard to minister to others when we have a lot of unresolved issues in our lives.

It's worth noting an important difference between a puddle of water that is still and still water that comes from flowing rivers. There are situations where the water is pure and not necessarily moving, but you still see flowing water coming through its way. This is the water that goes over rocks and becomes purified. It is the water that you see near waterfalls. The water you buy in the bottle is not contaminated.

The Almighty God understands there are times that our souls need to be refreshed. There are times when we're going to have to wash ourselves clean because we may have done some things that have made us a little dirty and filthy and hence, we need to be purified. God is not going to take us to a lake or to a swamp or to a puddle of water that formed from the rain and tell us, "Take a bath in there. Clean yourself up in there." He knows that we would come out dirtier and worse, and we may even come up with a fungus because green algae is contained in the water.

When you drive to Florida, there is a peculiar smell that says, "There's a swamp somewhere around here." But, the Almighty God doesn't lead us by the swamps. Even though the Florida swamps have still waters, what else comes along with the swamps? Alligators, snakes, bacteria, and other things that can cause death.

On the contrary, when God leads you by the still waters of rivers and waterfalls, you will experience things that are flourishing like fish and flowers. You may even see a deer because the Bible tells us, *"...the deer pants for the water."* You won't see any deer along the swampy water because deer run to where there is fresh water. They can only drink from the water that is not contaminated and that is free of alligators, snakes, bacteria among others. God leads us to the same type of still water and makes us lie down in the green pastures. But then, why are green pastures and still waters normally found together? It is simply because the pastures will continue to remain green when they are watered well. That's why the Bible teaches us in Psalm 1 that blessed is the man who *"shall be like a tree planted by the rivers of water."*

Jesus Is the Living Water

Another reason why the Almighty God takes us by the still waters that is connected to the living waters is simply because the rivers of living waters represent the person of Jesus Christ. Jesus is compared to living waters and as long as the living water is flowing, dead things cannot exist there. It is hard for living water to become contaminated because it is constantly flowing. God is always moving in your life to get rid of those things that are not right so that you can continuously lie down by the green pastures.

It's just like God is saying, "I am filtering you, and purifying you. I am alkalizing your body. I am alkalizing your spirit so that you know that I am God, and when things begin to arise in you that are not like me, you can automatically realize that something is not right and has to be flushed."

The difference between filtered water and tap water is clear. Tap water is not the real, fresh water; it has been processed by man. I don't care how many lemons you squeeze over in it, you still know it's not fresh water.

God is trying to take us by the still waters, where we can be refreshed. And once He leads us to these still waters, He can restore our souls. This is the assurance that we have based on the next verse of Psalm 23, which we will cover in the next chapter.

It takes His leading us to the still waters to get our souls restored, refreshed and revived by the riverside.

God Wants Us to Be Clean

When God is trying to lead you through the still waters, do not allow your response to be, "I'm good over here, I'm cool over here." Have you ever had to force a young child to take a bath? Sometime ago, I used to babysit a girl who was two years younger than me. I had the most challenging time getting her to take a bath, because she was scared of water. Even when she finally got into the bathtub, she would constantly repeat, "[Panting] I don't want to take a bath." I would give her a few minutes to bathe and then come back to check on her. The rag didn't smell like anything, because she put the rag in the water and took it out to make it look like she bathed — skin just as dry and gritty because she didn't like taking baths. I said, "No, you've got to break that habit. You are a girl and you need to be clean." This is exactly what God wants to do for us.

God wants us to be clean. We have been through some things, and if He doesn't clean us up very well, people are not going to recognize that God is our Shepherd. We have to give God the time He requires to work on the situations in our lives, so that others will not look at us and come to the unfortunate conclusion that God is not really a good Shepherd as Christians portray Him. Most times, because of the way we look, we lose others through our testimony – because we aren't restored. Our testimony, our victory over life's circumstances will draw others to Christ. At one point in my life, my Mama used to say, "I ain't never seen so many broke down Christians in my life!"

Hence, it is important for us to allow God to lead us to the still waters in order to be restored, refreshed, revived and renewed. Then, no matter the challenges that come our way, we will have the inner strength to rise against them and overcome them by the blood of the Lamb and by the words of our testimony — that testimony that God is our Shepherd and LORD can work wonders for us in the face of life's problems.

CHAPTER 3

The LORD
Restores and Leads Me

"He restoreth my soul: He leadeth me in the paths of righteousness for His name's sake." (Psalm 23:3)

After we are refreshed by God, He has to come and restore us, and He has to detoxify our lives. When I was a child, I was a handful, but my family worked with me to become a better person. God does the same thing with us. That's why He takes time to mold us into His greatness. The Bible tells us that we should *"fear not the man that can destroy our bodies, but rather fear the one that can destroy both the body and the soul."* In making God our LORD and Shepherd, we allow Him to do His job in breaking and building us back up. After restoring our soul, He will lead us in the path of righteousness for His name's sake. But then, what does "for His name's sake" mean?

God Takes 100% of the Risk

The Almighty God does everything for His good. God's greatness reveals to us that because we have made a covenant in making Him our LORD, He will do everything in His power to keep us from evil, *because His name is on the line.* So, you have nothing to lose if you hand over the control and administration of your life to Him. He is the risk taker - He wouldn't let anything taint His holy name. He doesn't want the enemy to make a mockery of His personality. If, for instance, wolves get into God's pastures and successfully hurt or harm a sheep there, the enemy would rejoice in victory over God's omnipotence. More so, the enemy would say that God is not really able to keep watch over His own people. But, God is forever able! God is faithful to what He has called to Himself. God's name is attached to us and because we call ourselves Christians, He will not allow us become the subjects of any evil thing. Thus, as followers of Christ, we have to set an example for the unbelievers because our lives hold a persuasive power in their call to salvation. God cleans and restores us in order to bring us to a place better than where we were before. He also gives us grace in time of difficulties so that we don't make a mockery of His name.

How can I believe on the God that you are serving when I can't see any benefits in your life? How can I believe God to bring me out of a bad marriage when your marriage is not good as well? Are you serious? You want me to believe God for something that didn't work in the same area of your life? If you're addicted to this and that and you want to tell me about your God being the deliverer, I don't see it. Hence, when we start testifying to people, we've got to make sure that we're the living proof of whatever we're testifying about in God. We also have to make sure that God has been made the LORD over that area of our life, that our souls have been restored in that aspect of our lives, and that we've been lying down in green pastures for a while in that area of our lives.

Once God restores our soul, once HE has recreated us, then what can He do? Lead us in the path of righteousness. Why? For His name's sake. God leads us so that we won't go back. He puts His name on the line because we've made Him our Shepherd. God has to lead the people whose souls He restores in the path of righteousness. He's not just going to lead you down any path; He has to lead you down the path of righteousness because His name is on the line. If we go around telling people that God is our Shepherd, He has to clean us up. You have to let go of everything that you were addicted to in the past. God will lead you by whatever means, because His name is attached to your life. You have to let it go because we don't have time to keep going back over our issues time and again.

Proof of Submission

We have to show that we've been tested, tried and approved by God, and that we are now a living proof of God being the LORD in every area of our lives. Otherwise, we begin to contradict ourselves whenever we have to minister to others, most especially unbelievers. How are you going to tell someone about divine healing when you're always seen with the same sickness over and over – not even a different one? I can understand if you got sick and God healed you, and when something else also happened, He healed you of that too. But, I think, you have no good story to tell if you become ill with the same thing over and over again. It is going to be hard for you to convince me, or anyone else that God is able to heal.

If we are living in the same situation, with both of our husbands beating us, how are you going to tell me that God wants peace in my house when you only have one black eye and I have two? How can you convince me?

For this reason, God has to show His rod and His staff to get you down this path of righteousness so as to protect His name. We signed an agreement with God, and according to verse one, He is the Shepherd and He will lead us by any means necessary because His name is attached to the agreement. Even though He's taking 100% of the risk in this covenant, He won't shy away from getting you into the place of submission so that, knowing or unknowingly, you won't soil His name.

We can't be "bootleg" Christians where all we know is to speak in tongues and holler and scream about – that adds no substance to our lives. My brother recently shared with me how he was talking to his landlord before he rented the property where he currently lives. The landlord said, "There were a lot of bishops, preachers, and pastors who wanted this house, but they wanted to put it in the church's name and make the church pay for it. Furthermore, they had other flimsy stuff going on. I did not get the impression that they were real bishops like you." God's Spirit, speaking by the mouth of Apostle Paul, complained about the life of the Israelites, saying, *"For the name of God is blasphemed among the Gentiles through you, as it is written,"* (See Romans 2:24) People can see the truth. People can see God. And, people can see a form of godliness. So do you have God or a form of godliness? Are you one that knows all the language and the lingo to use, or are you the one who just does it...you live the life?

God's Name Is Stamped on Your Life

The Almighty God has His name stamped on your life and He actually took time to tattoo your name in the palm of His hands. He is therefore going to slap you with His hand and bring you down this road of righteousness by whatever means he deems fit to deal with you, if, in any case, you want to go astray.

One time I slapped a light skinned boy. Let me tell you, that was a funny day in the Davis family. Some of our friends were over and he just kept talking. Everybody knew I was a tomboy when I was growing up and I would fight boys and anybody else. I was like, "move it along...move it along." He just kept talking, and he thought he was funny. Well, I already had enough, so I took my hand and smacked him across the face. After I slapped him, you could literally see my thumb and all my fingers in his face. My whole hand was on his face. I said, "I told you to leave me alone."

Sometimes, God has to treat us in the same manner. He has to smack us at times so that we will get back in line. The Bible tells us, stating, "...*he who the Lord loves, He chastises*" (See Hebrews 12:6). Whom He loves, He'll go hunting after. He'll leave everyone else to find you. Number one, you have to be willing to be found. And number two, you must be willing to go down the path that He's leading. I promise you His path may not seem as beautiful as other paths, but it's not as rough. Why? Of course, He is with you. Sometimes, people think living holy is hard, but living in sin is hard and expensive.

For example, cheating on your "boo" is expensive. I told somebody I don't see how he could have three or four girlfriends at the same time, because it was an expensive thing to do. It already cost a lot being the only one and he had four girlfriends. Are you serious? Sinning is expensive; it will cost you a lot. Addictions are expensive, they will cost you great things. On the other hand, living for God only costs you to *sacrifice* yourself. Living for God will only cause you to sacrifice so that in the end your soul may be saved. But when you learn to give up some of those addictions...to give up that sinful life...to give up other things that have got you down, you will find that you have more money in your pocket, more happiness in your heart, and a peace that *"surpasses all understanding."* (See Philippians 4:7)

You Must Trust God

You can't tell God, "God, I'm trusting you with this area," but then when you get worried, you will determine that it's hard, and then, you decide to drink your problems away, or smoke your problems away, or sip a little, puff a little or drag a little bit. Rather than doing these things, you need to be confessing that you trust God.

In the same vein, if you've had problems with your marriage for a while, you need to renew your mind before the Lord, your Shepherd. You're just like, "LORD I'm going to trust you with my marriage. I'm not going to touch him or her; I'm just going to look. I'm not going to do anything; I'm just going to take a peek." One foot is going one way, because you see God leading you that way, but you have your other foot going another way. Impossible. Curiosity killed what? It killed the cat. Be stable in your decision - the agreement you have with God.

Now, you see God leading you down the path of righteousness – He's taking you through the Red Sea and the water is filling up, but you are getting uncomfortable. Before you know it, you start tripping over on another path. You must stay on the path that God has ordained for you. You will be safe there. You will find refuge there. Everything you need is there. You have to let God lead you on the path of righteousness; you will not fail because His name is attached to it.

I refuse to go through the wilderness if my soul is not restored. I refuse to go through challenging situations and remain dehydrated. I refuse to go through and remain weak and worn out. When I go through life alone, I will have no strength, I will have no hope, I will have no energy, I will not have my family, and I will not have God to guide me. I refuse to go through this situation by myself. Since you, a mortal being, can't predict the events of time and seasons, you need someone greater than you, who can lead you through so that you won't be a victim of circumstances.

I have to allow the LORD to lead me to the righteous path and I have to allow Him to lead me by the waters so that He can make sure that I'm hydrated. Even Jesus had enough sense to do that. After being tempted in the wilderness by the devil, Jesus had enough sense to allow the angels to minister to Him before He went out into the world. (See Matthew 4:1-11) He had to make sure His strength was renewed, He had to make sure that His mindset was right. Because He was weak, He was vulnerable - so He wouldn't go out there to fulfill the Father's mandate without first getting restored and refreshed, and hence the need for that angelic visitation.

What Would You Decide?

Most often, we take our weak and vulnerable selves out there, trying to do work for the LORD and we eventually become defeated by the shadows of death. We then become devoured by evil, because we did not take time to rest in the presence of God. We didn't take time to read the Word of God and set our eyes upon the Word. We didn't take time in prayer to let God restore our soul; we stepped out there and now we are overtaken. I refuse to be like that. If I'm going to die, I'm going to die with the reality that I did everything that God told me to do. If I'm going to die, it's because God says it's just time for me to go. I don't want to die physically or spiritually when God has not given death the permission.

I must live for God, I have to live for myself, I have to live for my husband, I have to live for my children, and I have to live for the church. There is a part of me that wants to make up for all the lies that false Christians have spread around the world. There's a part of me that has to stay alive. There is a part of me that has to help bring sanctification back to the cross. There's a part of me spiritually that has to bring back reverence to Jesus Christ – to make people understand that without Christ in my life, without the LORD leading me along the path of righteousness, I am but nothing. John the Baptist said, "*He must increase, but I must decrease.*" (John 3:30). That is, Christ must be all in all as far as my life is concerned.

CHAPTER 4

The LORD
Removes My Fears &
Comforts Me

"Yea, though I walk through the valley of the shadow of death, I will fear no evil: for thou art with me; thy rod and thy staff they comfort me." (Psalm 23:4)

There are times that we are going to walk through the valley of the shadow of death when God is leading us. We are not walking through death; instead, we are walking through the valley and we may experience the shadow of death. What is a shadow? It's an illusion, a figure that's created by another object. What does the shadow represent? It's a warning. There's a connection between shadow of death and evil. Evil is the real thing, the actual entity, while the shadow is the warning that something evil is coming.

The Importance of Light

David told us not to fear evil and not to fear the shadow of death. We learned that a shadow can't be present without light. Light has to be available for a shadow to be visible, seen, or revealed. God, as our Shepherd, sends us a warning that evil things are coming by exposing the evil entity's shadow. The problem with us is that we ignore the shadow; therefore, we ignore the warning. And because we ignore the Holy Spirit who revealed Christ and sin unto us, we become afraid of evil.

Jesus Himself was the Light; yet He walked in the light of His Father. And so, He did not ignore the Holy Spirit. That was why He was never afraid of evil. He even said, "*The prince of this world cometh, and hath nothing in me.*" (John 14:30). Christ had conquered evil before it even came to Him, for the Father had earlier exposed the evil through the shadow it cast by virtue of the light of God.

God will not send us into war without giving us strategies, but instead of looking over the book that provides the strategies, we ignore the warnings and remain unprepared. We should not ignore the warning signs in our journey through the valley of the shadow of death, but rather recognize the Light that is with us.

God is the Light that is with us and because He is with us, we are privy to the enemy's plans and we can take comfort in the Light and become overcomers. Whether we are in the valley or on the mountain, as long as God is there with us, we should be thankful that His light is still with us. So even when the devil tries to come in like a flood, the light of God is so big and bright that it creates a shadow of the enemy's plan and reveals it unto us. *"When the enemy shall come in like a flood, the Spirit of the Lord shall lift up a standard against him."* (Isaiah 59:19)

The Bible tells us that the *"devil comes not but to steal, to kill and to destroy."* (See John 10:10). Since shadow can only be created if the object is in the light, hence, it is obvious that light and darkness have to be near each other at some point. In order for the shadow to be exposed, light has to be present. God is the light that reveals to you the plot that the enemy has against your life. God has to be present to expose the enemy.

That is why we can foresee the coming of the enemy before he even strikes. This is the reason why the enemy thought he was going to take us, but God came in and we saw the shadow.

> *Through the tender mercy of our God; whereby*
> *the dayspring from on high hath visited us, To*
> *give light to them that sit in darkness and in*

the shadow of death, to guide our feet into the
way of peace. (Luke 1:78-79)

The reason the devil can't win in my life is because God has already exposed him before he can come on the scene and cause any harm. Just because he comes to kill, steal and destroy, doesn't mean he gets to kill, steal and destroy – he has been exposed by the omniscient, Almighty God.

Do Not Be Afraid of the Shadow

I want to make sure you understand this: you'll see the shadow before you see the wicked plans of the enemy. Therefore, before the enemy can come in and try to overtake, I have already seen him a mile away. God has already shone His great big light on the enemy, thus creating a shadow that I can see from afar. If I'm walking down the path and all of a sudden I see this big, black spot beside me, I know it's not supposed to be there. Instead of trying to fight the shadow, I need not fear, but to apply faith in prayer.

A woman at our ministry once told me that she and her husband started arguing and fussing and they didn't normally do that. She told her husband, "Hold on. We have to stop because something isn't right; something is abnormal about this situation. We are doing stuff that we don't do in our household." It was time to pray because she saw the shadow. She saw what the devil was trying to slide in to destroy that area of her life. But, she didn't get scared and say, "Oh God what is this thing that's trying to come upon me? What is this thing?" She didn't fear; she kept on moving and she applied her faith through prayer.

Sometimes, we see the shadow and we lose our courage. When we see the water is pulled back, the next thing we believe is that the shark is coming along to get us. The greatest picture of the parting of the Red Sea I've ever seen was in the movie - *The Prince of Egypt*. Eventually, when the Red Sea was parted in the movie, fishes and whales were going through the water on one side and were still moving. Sometimes we see what's in the water and we say, "Oh my God, there's a shark...oh my God, there's a whale...oh my God, there's a jellyfish...oh my God, there's a stingray." We are freaking out, even though those things that can harm us have all been pushed back. The presence of God is before us. Of course, we may see the shadow of the fish that is pushed back as we are walking on dry land, we should stay in faith that God will guide us in safety.

At times, the devil tries to tell us, "You think you got God with you this time, but I'm coming back. You think you made it through this time, but I'm going back. You think you're going to beat this addiction, but I've got another one for you. Now, see what you can do for that. You thought you overcame cancer, I've got something else for you." The most unfortunate thing you could ever do is to listen and give heed to the devil. Whose voice would you believe? The Good Shepherd or the enemy? (See John 10: 4-5)

You should not fear any evil. Why is the shadow of death compared to evil? It's darkness; it's sin. It is from the enemy. Even though the valley of the shadow of death is evil, we should not be fearful because God is with us. Many times, I've heard people say to someone in big trouble, "You're going through death." That's the opinion of man. You're not

47

in any way going through death. Stop letting people speak things into your life that are not even in the Word. *That* thing is not going to kill you. It's a shadow, and God is trying to give you a warning beforehand. God gives us warnings about what's to come so we know how to go on and pray. That's why we have the Holy Spirit; He reveals things to us. He shows us what needs to be done to keep an evil thing from happening; and if it does happen, we understand how to go through it because God is always there. The Bible says, *"And we know that all things work together for good to them that love God, to them who are the called according to his purpose."* (Romans 8:28)

Is the Shadow My Own Reflection?

God is forever true and faithful. That is why I understand that even if I'm the reflection of the shadow, that is, if I'm walking and I see my own shadow, it simply means I need to re-evaluate myself before I continue to go through this valley. I might need to be restored again so that I won't see a reflection of myself. Therefore, I would cease to be afraid of the death that I see within myself, because God has exposed it to me. Moreover, I know every time God reveals my issues to other people, I have to allow Him to expose my shadows of death and evil to me through the individual He may want to use to help me. In any case, I have to stop and check myself. One thing is sure - God will allow His light to shine on me and purge me because I surrender to the light. (See II Corinthians 13:5)

I am thankful that as we go on the journey of life, through the wilderness of this world, God deems it apt to reveal unto us the shadows of ourselves – the sin that we didn't let go, which necessitated the purging our lives at the place of still waters. He will always take definite steps to address those issues that we think we've overcome, but from which we really haven't been delivered because we haven't been tempted in some time. In other words, the sin problem is beneath the flesh, waiting for a time to pull us down. God must deal with them before those things adversely deal with us. Even in that process of divine brokenness, God is there with us. He's telling us that even through the longest valley, He is there guiding us through so that we can overcome. The thing that burdens you will not be the thing that takes you out, but you must heed the warnings.

Let God Detoxify Your Life

Whenever God shows me my own shadows, He is simply revealing my own flaws, my own imperfections. This act helps me grow in the faith, and it also serves as a spiritual detox in my life, reconnecting me back to that still water to which God leads me. God's Word is water - it can cleanse the spirit, the soul and the body. So, it's not reserved for spiritual cleansing alone; the water can detoxify your body as well. (See Proverbs 4:22)

What's the first thing that begins to happen when you detoxify your body and alkalize it? Pimples and boils tend to come because the body is trying to release those toxins that are part of your life. You begin to poop a lot and your poop has a stench that goes along with it. Those things that were not right in your life are gone. Sometimes, you may see little worms and white eggs in your stool. You can thank God that those worms are gone too. That infestation is being released, and you might not eat that again if it's going to require this type of result in your body. In the same vein, when we drink from the still waters, we can be sure that the water goes into every fiber of our being and washes out all those impurities. We may see a bump here, but we pop it and get rid of it. We may see a rash there, but we apply ointment to it and get rid of it.

When people look at you and they ask, "Baby, what's going on with your face," you can say, "I'm detoxifying myself. God is revealing some things to me about myself that I'm working on. Be patient with me. I asked God to rid me of the stuff that isn't right. When I allowed Him to be LORD, He came in and He just took over and I have no control over what's happening in my body. All I know is that I feel good. I feel healthier, and I feel happy in the peace of God."

You'll be full of thanks to God when you see tangible changes such that you begin to say things like: "I don't see my shadow," or "My shadow is not as big as it used to be. When I walked in the past, my shadow used to be this big. Now, it's all gone. I can only see myself. I see myself with God because I submitted to God's detox beside the still waters."

Do Not Allow Fear to Overtake Your Faith

Personally, I didn't feel afraid when I was trying to lose weight in my flesh, because I allowed God to help me gain confidence. Jealousy and envy made me gain weight. I finally started letting go of negative thoughts, because I became confident in myself and who I was in God. I didn't have to prepare myself to dry out and didn't have to put my husband down to make myself look better.

When God shines His light on your situation, He'll make it look like: I may not be the smartest person in my class, but God has given me gifts and talents to take me a long way. I might be big and others may be small, but I know that my God saved me.

Therefore, I'm not afraid of myself, I'm not afraid of the future, and I'm not afraid to go through the Red Sea, because I know I'm going to come out. Passing through the valley of the shadow of death will cause you to re-evaluate your life, and I refuse to step through the valley to get to the mountain unless I've truly had a cleansing from the LORD.

There is a song that says, "The blood that gives me strength, from day to day, it will never lose its power…it reaches to highest mountain, it flows to lowest valley." The blood of Jesus Christ has enough power to reach you whether you're at your highest point or at your lowest juncture. David's writing helps us understand that at some point we are going to have to go through the valley, but because the light from God is so strong, it will illuminate every evil plot that the devil has planned against our lives. We don't have to be afraid; no matter the weapons the enemy has formed against us, they shall not prosper. God has already exposed the hand of the enemy. The only way they could prosper is by ignoring the signs and warnings that God gives concerning them.

If you allow fear to overtake your faith and you get comfortable with walking in the valley, complaining and doubting, you have voided the agreement you signed with God when you made Him your Shepherd. However, God understands that sometimes it gets hard and the shadows can be overwhelmingly big. All the same, He's with you!

The Comfort after the Chastening

God understands how His children operate. The Word says, *"Thy rod and staff, they comfort me."* (See Psalm 23:4) What is the purpose of the rod and staff? God will use them to bring you back to where you belong, because there is too much potential in you for you to sit around a valley. The Bible tells us that *'a rod is for a fool's backside'* (See Proverbs 6:3), *'spare the rod, spoil the child'* (See Proverbs13:24) *and 'whom the Lord loves, he chastens.'* (See Hebrews 12:6)

There is no joy in using the rod or staff, but its beauty is found in what comes after it has been used. The beauty that comes after God comforts you is in knowing what is to be avoided so as to also avoid the chastisement. The comfort results from God "beating" the issues out of our lives, thereby making us better people. He loves you with an everlasting love, and He means well for you. You can take comfort in knowing that the thing that had you bound will no longer hold its power over you because the Potter loved you enough to break and build you back up on a continuous cycle until you overcame. At some point, we should want to be free enough to heed the warnings, read the plans, and let God liberate us from the valley. At some point, we need to get on the mountain and soar like an eagle. We need to see ourselves grow greater, and if that comes from letting God's rod and staff comfort us, so be it.

His rod and His staff comfort us, but some people try to make the rod and staff majestic. No, the rod and staff are just used for different purposes. A rod is used to spank your butt back in; a staff is used to hook you and pull you back on track – even if it means breaking your legs. The best way to put it is that the comfort doesn't come until the rod and staff have been applied because the Bible tells us that the LORD chastises those He loves. So, once God chastises you and deals with those situations you're going through, then you can find comfort in Him. Just like it isn't fun getting your tail beaten by your momma and daddy, it isn't fun being whooped by God. But after the whooping, you learn your lesson and you'll never do it again unless you're a fool. Take the comfort and learn the lesson.

You Are Anointed by Experience

Now it's amazing that God has to go through a process with us before He is able to anoint for His use. He has to make sure that the blemish is gone. He has to make sure that we can take corrections and that we understand our place – not just in life, but in Him. He has to find us worthy to know that we're overcomers. He needs to find us worthy and understand that we can submit to His leadership and His Lordship. Once He realizes that we are of good quality, He anoints us for our task - anything we need to do within the context of His sovereign will. (See Hebrews 1:9)

Some people are really talented when ministering to women. Why? It's because they've been there; they have been through that battle. They have experienced some things in their life, and the experience qualifies them to be anointed with that gift - being a seasoned counselor in a help ministry. Because God says, "Okay, they understand the process that someone else needs to go through, and they didn't sit in the valley of the shadow of death and just wallow and stay there. They got up; they kept moving because I'm a moving God. I've had to correct them, I've had to teach them how to

53

forgive, how to love, how to do this and that. I had to allow certain situations to happen when they came face to face with the enemy; they didn't compromise in any way. They stood in front of their enemies, antagonists, and they didn't rain curses on them, but rather, they showed love. They passed every test. And as a result, she should be anointed to minister in that particular area, because there is experience attached to it."

We want to be anointed in areas where we have no experience. I would not make a good doctor, but I make an excellent teacher. But, we have to understand that God has anointed us for a particular thing in life. My momma always used to tell me, "Whatever thing you appoint yourself to, you have to anoint yourself for it. Dana, a member of our ministry, wanted to be a nurse, and I told her, 'How are you going be a nurse if you don't like the sight of throw up or blood? I'm confused.' She said, 'But I want to work with babies.' They poop and vomit the most. At the sight of blood, she freaks out. How is she going to work in a hospital? I encouraged her to stick to teaching." On a particular day, I went to watch Dana and others dance, and this one girl came in and was determined she was going be a dancer, but every movement got worse and worse. At the end of the performance, I encouraged the girl to maximize her poetic gift and encouraged her to do spoken, poetic rhymes and the likes. In this case, she wouldn't need to do movement, because she has not been anointed for that thing. The truth need be told; get in your lane and drive where God has told you to go. That's all!

When you go through things in your life, God uses those experiences to be a service to others. You just don't go through the valley of the shadow of death because you're just going through. You're going through because God is trying to prepare you for a mission. He's trying to anoint you for a mission. (See II Corinthians 1:3-6)

I never could understand why God would allow to me to go from finding my father at home in the bed dead to my mother dying, and to seeing several people die – being in a hospital room and seeing someone die right in front of my face. I kept saying to myself, "Are you serious?" I never really understood why God began to take me through those things, but when I became a Pastor, it all began to make sense. Because of what I went through, I was now equipped to minister to children who didn't have both parents. I was equipped to minister to single mothers who don't know how they're going to raise their children on their own, all because I saw my mother go through it.

I could have taken all the things I went through as a punishment, because I thought God didn't love me or He had an issue with me. Why me? Why me? It even came to a point when I said, "I'm good to my momma and daddy; why you had to take them from me? And this other girl is rebellious, why can't you take her parents; she clearly doesn't appreciate them. And you had to take my parents." God's response to me was, "I'm giving others time to get it together."

God Is Qualified to Anoint You

The Almighty is a gracious God and He has a tendency to answer me sarcastically when I question Him.

Just like He asked Job, *"Where were you when I formed this earth?"* In other words, God was saying, "Excuse me boo, you didn't come until thousands of years later and you want to question my being God, my loyalty, and why I allow things to happen to you?"

God is overly qualified. He has got this. Basically, it goes back to the first verse, *"the LORD is my Shepherd, I shall not want."* But I came to understand that every situation that God took me through wasn't a punishment. I can't have a testimony unless I've had a test. I have to overcome something in order to be considered an overcomer. If I am going to teach on forgiveness, I have to have a life of forgiveness. I tell people the way you know you've forgiven a person is when you stop avoiding being confronted with that person. I can tell you I've forgiven you all day long and never see you another day in my life.

How do I know if I've fully forgiven you in my heart unless I'm confronted face to face with you? I know I've forgiven you if my heart still feels good around you and I'm able to tell you that I love you and I mean it. So, what we have to begin to do in our minds is to stop using the trials and tribulations that we've been through as the rationale behind why we can't do anything for God. Rather, we should allow Him to use us as He deems fit.

Not all our trials are a rationale for our actions. "Well, you know it's been hard all my life. My dog died on my 21st birthday. My momma died on Mother's Day." What does that have to do with the price of oil? We try to justify the present things by something that happened in the past. For example, a man refuses to be nice to women because a woman from his past broke his heart. Women, we are not off the hook either. Some women say, "All men cheat, all men are dogs, and they are no good." When the Almighty God tries to bless you with the person that will make you happier and you have trust issues, you'll foolishly block your blessing, because you refuse to come out and say this thing was hard, but I got through it. Like my momma used to say "It didn't kill you. So, if it didn't kill you, it made you stronger and wiser to deal with that situation in the future."

We have to allow God to anoint us to the calling that He's placed upon our lives. Ask God why He put you in this position? Take lessons from what you've been through and remember that certain things make some things better. I never understood why teenage girls flocked to me to ask me for advice. God told me that I was anointed for just that, so I walked in it. You have to know what you're anointed for. For example, one of the mothers in our church has an anointing for hugs. It's there with no strings attached, no attitude, no faces – just love. Some people have an anointing for encouragement. It's hard sometimes and even so often we need a word or two to help us get back on our feet and to remind us of the goodness of God. We are anointed to do certain things because we must have learned wisdom and counsel through our personal experience, and God Himself notices we are able to handle being a witness to others in that area. For example, there are some people who are anointed to give when they see others in need. So ask God what He has anointed you to do? Whether it's preaching, teaching, giving, encouraging, dancing, hugging, serving, we must do it well because HE has prepared us for the task at hand.

57

Believe it or not, only the LORD, the Shepherd, knows who you are. You don't know yourself. He made you; He's allowed you to be shaped by various life's challenges so that you can fit into a definite part of His purpose for the Church and humanity. Even, Jesus Himself, the only begotten Son of JEHOVAH, learned obedience (submission to the Father's leadership and will) by yielding to God's dealings with Him as regards those things He suffered. What was the Father's intent? It was to anoint Him for service, to make Him become the Captain of eternal salvation to believers, and to make Him bring many sons and daughters to glory. (See Hebrews 2:10, 5:7-9) Allow your Shepherd to lead you all the way. He knows the best for your life. Walk in that anointing you've received from your LORD because of all of your experiences – those you consider both favorable and unfavorable.

CHAPTER 5

The LORD
Purifies & Anoints Me

"Thou preparest a table before me in the presence of mine enemies: thou anointest my head with oil; my cup runneth over." (Psalm 23:5)

Next, the Bible says that God prepares a table before us in the presence of our enemies. (See Psalm 23:5) We should be delighted that God sends us through a process, because He will never put us before our enemies, leaving us there to feel miserable or neglected. God makes sure that we are fully armed and ready to face our enemies. It may be ten years before God puts you before your enemies again, but when the time comes, your mindset will be renewed and unbothered with confidence in the One who delivered you. You are then ready to spoil the stronghold of the wicked and recover the wealth kept there.

The Bible tells us that *"the wealth of the wicked is stored up for the righteous,"* and that He has to lead the righteous down the right path. (See Proverbs 13:22) He goes further to say, *"Vengeance is mine; I will repay, saith the Lord"* (See Romans 12:19-21) We must be aware that nobody can avenge us of our enemies like the Almighty God would do.

When God gives you the satisfaction of making your enemies come back to say, "I'm sorry," it is the best compensation you could ever get. How could God revive you and reassure you that you are more than an overcomer, if you refuse to overcome? The Bible tells us that we overcome by the blood of the Lamb, then the testimony comes. If we continue to allow the same mindset of the valley hold us down, we won't experience the reality of the table being prepared for us.

Now, who is your enemy? An enemy is anything that is against the will of God in your life. It could be habits, addictions, and other vices. In fact, some of your friends are actually your enemies because they have no good wishes for you in life. And if you haven't gone through God's purification process, you are going to give in to the wiles of those enemies until you have overcome. In order to allow God to prepare a table before you while your enemies just look on, you have to separate yourselves from those vices and the circumstances that promote them in your life. For instance, if you have a problem with drugs, stay away from the drug house and break the evil habit. Until you recognize what your enemy really is, you will never be able to subdue it. Besides, God will not prepare a table before you until you are purged of *that* thing that always displeases Him. When you're confronted face to face by such a thing, which is the trouble in your very life, and you overcome it, you will know that you have the victory. Nevertheless, you have to be honest with yourself on this confrontation.

You have to make sure that you smell nice, have on the right attire, and are ready to present yourself in decency and in order. It begins with changing the mindset. You have to make sure there isn't still a part of you that has not been purged from the enemy. At the table, your enemies have to bring something to you for all of your pain and suffering. They have to invest back into your life. That is, God will make sure that you receive what you lost plus interest. However, don't sit around waiting on your enemy to pay you back, go through the process to get healed, and let God handle the recovery and restoration of all you might have lost while under the tyranny of evil. (See Joel 2:25, Psalm 126:1)

Don't let your enemies see you dilapidated. Look like God is your Lord, your Shepherd, and the Maker of all the

Earth. Be prepared at all times. You aren't only representing yourself, you're also standing in defense of the power in the blood of Jesus. You should be a living proof that the blood works. The scripture says, *"Thou prepares a table before me, in the presence of my enemies. Thou anoints my head with oil and my cup runneth over."*

Identifying the Enemy

Let's focus on the first part of the scripture, *"Thou prepares a table before me in the presence of my enemies."* You need to know the dos and don'ts when getting prepared to face your enemy. What is an enemy? An enemy is someone who is against you, someone who has set out to do you harm, someone who tries to get you in trouble. An enemy is anything or anyone who comes up against you or God in any kind of way. Many people today just think that their enemies are just human beings like them. It's more than that. An enemy can come in many forms: dogs, addictions, food, pride, sickness, your own thoughts, and sometimes you could be your own worst enemy. Your enemy could also be pride, laziness, bills, fears, addictions, money, etc. What I like about this scripture is that it simply tells us what God has done. Psalms 18:48 says, *"He delivereth me from mine enemies: yea, thou liftest me up above those that rise up against me: thou hast delivered me from the violent man."* When the scripture says that God *"delivereth us from our enemies,"* it simply implies that He destroys things that keep us from doing what He has called us to do. Sometimes we get so wrapped up in everyone else's deliverance that we do not allow God to deliver us from our own enemy. My momma used to say, "I want more for you than you want for yourself.

I can see you free, but you can't see yourself free." For example, when we talk about healing in the church, we must believe that God can heal us from the enemy called sickness or disease. (See Psalm 103:3)

Authority over the Enemy

Immediately God delivers you from your enemies; what does He do? He raises you up over the enemy. Why do you think God raises you up above those things? God puts you at a place of authority over them. The world tries to keep us down in immaturity, while God is there to raise you up in maturity. Sometimes God will have you walk over your enemies and sometimes God will raise you up over them where they can't have access to you and overtake you. Some people don't do well in combat against the enemy when they are trying to fight for their lives. Instead of knowing who they are in God before they attack, they become defeated. They develop a victim mentality complex: *everyone is out to get me and set me up for failure.* They don't realize that God wants to deliver them from the enemy and raise them up above those things so they can be triumphant. God lifts us up over our enemy so that we can look down and remember where He brought us from.

Renew Your Mind

In view of the foregoing, you must understand that victory begins in the mind. As a matter of fact, the mind is the major battleground from where your enemy attacks you. Your own thoughts can be your worst enemy if you haven't given God authority to renew your mind - that's a sure way to gain the authority over your enemies. It's no wonder the word of God instructs you, as an individual, to *"be renewed in the spirit of your mind."* (Ephesians 4:23) The quality of your mind determines whether you'll get victory or defeat as an outcome of your own thoughts.

The Bible is like a big puzzle wherein you need to gather the pieces together to obtain specific solutions to your problems. For example, people who have addiction issues need to know that they have the power to have a hold over the addiction and be victorious. At some point, you must realize you have been equipped; you can take back the authority the enemy has stolen from you. See, the enemy does not even want you to know that you have the authority to ward off the evil darts he keeps firing at your mind so as to keep you in perpetual bondage. That's why you are always musing on the problem, *"I can't help it. I just can't break off this thing!"* No. Don't think you can't do it. With God, you can! Get it right in your mind first. (See II Corinthians 10:3-6)

Yes, God will give you wise strategies to deal with your enemies. He will never keep you in the midst of your enemies without protection. Sometimes we'll be so focused on the enemy that we neglect the Victor inside of us. That's where we often have issues with the Shepherd. We put so much focus on the enemy that we unconsciously lessen the power of God in our lives. He can't prepare a table before us if we're stuck with our enemies. He can never consider us faultless in our disposition toward Him, if we constantly control our every movement. *"I can't do this"* and *"I won't go there"* are some of the holds of paranoia the enemy places on our minds to keep us bound. Take some solace in the testimony of David who knew firsthand that the God of Israel was good enough to be his Shepherd; he confessed, saying, *"God has delivered me and put me over my enemies."*

Deliverance from the Enemy

What is a violent man? Someone or something that wants to destroy you: loneliness, depression, gluttony, stress, etc. You want something better for yourself, but you never see yourself past this situation, past this relationship, past this way of thinking you can never be loved. It doesn't work that way. Sometimes you're the one that creates enemies for yourself. Even though God wants to remove them, you keep calling them back. Thus, you make yourself the victim of the violent man, and then you wonder why you are trapped within yourself. You become stuck and stagnant, not wanting to deal with the issues of your own self. You therefore can't put the blame on others when, in most cases, you are doing the harm to yourself. You even complain and discredit some of the positive things in your life and then murmur when you are lonely and depressed.

In order to have friends, you must show ourselves friendly. It's the Word of God. You have to get past our emotions. In the spiritual walk with Christ, your emotions and flesh will get in the way of the spirit. If you prioritize and rearrange your emotions, you can see, hear, and follow God in a clearer dimension. The Bible already reveals that your wrestle is primarily not against flesh and blood, and so you can't make everything a flesh and blood situation. In Ephesians 6:12, we are told that *our biggest enemies are spiritual things* – things in the atmosphere, things that exalt themselves against the power of God. It all starts in the spirit realm, then it tries to push its way to manifestation in the lives of people. But if you are on the alert, awake, and prayerful, God will transport you into the spirit realm to recognize when the enemy is trying to manipulate you and others.

God has eliminated some of your enemies from our very presence, but you're still bound by what they did even though they're gone. He's trying to help you move forward by lifting you up, removing the enemy, setting you on solid ground. Yet, you still live in the past hurt. But let me tell you something, as long as you live, there will be hurt; some people won't like you, some people want to see you fail and will set traps for you. It's part of the experience of life - it's highly inevitable. As long as there is a devil, there will be demons, trials, and tribulations. However, we have hope in the revelation that God will lift, deliver, and remove us from the attack of violent man.

Maybe, as of today, you're trying to get to the table that's being prepared for you in the presence of your enemies, but you're still tied down, being controlled by these bad things around you. Your enemies quickly take your attention away from God and replace it with worry and anxiety. That's why God tells you that you have to take captive every thought and imagination that is not part of His will. You have to pray and break yourself loose from the hold the enemy has put on you. At some point, you have to get it together.

Pray for God to Stop the Enemy Completely

Once you allow God to eliminate your enemy, you'll begin to experience God's work against the thing that has been the thorn in your flesh. Remember, your enemy could be someone or something that wants to destroy you, or a thing about your life, such as health, finance and marriage. There are things that God doesn't want you to do regarding your enemies - human beings specifically. Proverbs 24:17-18 says, *"Rejoice not when thine enemy falleth, and let not thine heart be glad when he stumbleth: Lest the Lord see it and it displease him, and he turn away his wrath from him."*

If you have trouble with a human enemy, you should know that it's your duty to call on God for deliverance, while it's God's own part to judge and remove the enemy from you. Therefore, whenever you pray for the downfall of your enemies, God will deliver you and destroy them. But then, if you rejoice in their demise, and God will halt His wrath. It's important to know that we can rejoice in God being a deliverer, we can celebrate that God has delivered us, but not that God has allowed our enemies to be drowned in the Red Sea. We can celebrate the greatness of God.

The sad thing to note is that if some persons are your enemies, they will also be enemies to someone else. The thing to do is pray that God stops the enemy completely. How? It's by changing the heart of the people and removing the evil spirit manipulating them. God wants us to learn that we must pray for our enemies. We should ask God to reset our mind on how we view them in our minds, thereby guarding us against the tendency of mocking them when they eventually fall for our sake.

Do you also know that when the enemy realizes he no longer holds power over you, he'll move along to the next person? The enemy is sitting around looking for people to torment, and though God has placed a hedge of protection over your life, pray for people that go blindly into the enemy's camp, who do not have the strength and the wherewithal to fight the enemy...perhaps who are even comfortable sitting on the enemy's lap.

It is sometimes amusing that when gamblers gamble away all their money, they make a prayer that if the next slot machine delivers a miracle, they won't gamble anymore. Most of the time, when they win, the spirit over their lives encourages them to continue gambling. You can't get comfortable in playing the hand of God when He's trying to deliver you. When God delivers you from the enemy, you can't keep running back to it. When God delivers you, allow Him to do so fully, and don't make a mockery of God's deliverance. If, for instance, you know you have been delivered from alcoholism, don't go to the bar anymore. We often put ourselves in situations that will make it easy to relapse into bondage after having received God's deliverance. It requires some working effort to keep the deliverance that God has bestowed upon you. You're not a superhuman. The enemy will set traps to instantly degrade the power of God, and then we wonder why we have a victim mentality complex in those aspects of our lives.

Overcoming the Enemy

In times of rainy seasons, especially when God has delivered you from your enemies, you can't expect to be a champion and be able to save the world when you're infants in your deliverance. You have to give it time before you can share your experience with everyone about how to do it right. Sometimes, we cannot celebrate our victories too soon until we know that God has done the complete work in us. You cannot prematurely talk about your deliverance, until you've been fully delivered and refilled with the power and Spirit of God. So, when you are faced with those issues, you can walk away. When you walk away each time you are faced with such issues, then you can take that as a sign that you've overcome the thing. If you give in to it, you're still its captive.

I don't mess with hookahs. I have never smoked a day in my life. I haven't smoked a blunt, weed, cigarette, and pipes because I don't like their odor. If you have a smoking problem, don't play around with hookahs, even though they're not nicotine. If you used to be a weed head, don't experiment because it opens up doors in your lives that were closed; and it brings back the *spirit of familiarity*, before it becomes a black and mild Marlboro, then it's weed, and before you know it, you have fallen right back into the hands of the enemy. We must shut the door completely.

Live under God's protection, because if you keep playing around with it, you'll have to deal with it on your own if God removes his hands. We play games with the devil too much. We ask God to give us an escape with bills, but we spend the money on shopping. That's the enemy. If you set plans, stick to them. Are we supposed to enjoy the fruit of our labor? Yes. But there are times when we are trying to be free from the enemies so that we can fully enjoy them, so stop this *pre-enjoying* lifestyle and accept your responsibility. We should aim to build something that will last.

The Bible teaches us that we become slaves to the ones we borrow from. God is trying to get us to a position where our past can't haunt us. We have to get ourselves together and deal with the little monsters in our closet. We have to clear our minds. If you know you're weak with money, give it to someone who can invest and save it for you. If you're not good with something, keep your hands off it, until you learn how to handle it. Whatever controls all your thoughts, stay away from it.

We cannot be wealthy physically and spiritually, then a few months later be broke again. We must have control over the things that want to control us. How can you control the things of God, if you cannot control your flesh? Ask God to help you get yourself together. He has rescued you from other enemies, now ask Him to help you from yourself, your worst enemy. Leave the things that will destroy you alone. Apply wisdom so that you can stay free.

Abundance from the Shepherd

Let's look at the last part of verse five, *"my cup runneth over."* What does that statement mean? It means abundance. What is your cup? Your cup is your life, your needs, your storehouses – any place that you've allowed God to empty and fill it back up with His own fullness. Abundance will show up if you are walking in God's anointing. You can't expect abundance to flow in areas of your life that God has not anointed and where His blood hasn't been appropriated.

It goes back to sowing seeds. For instance, if you haven't been sowing kind seeds and love seeds, you can't expect those things to come back to you. You have a hard time giving? You cannot expect a flow of abundance with people sowing into your life. You can't expect that "cup" in your life to be productive when you haven't been sowing the right seeds. You say, "Every time I see this or that person, he doesn't smile at me." Well, do you smile at people when you walk in the room? You will miss a lot of blessings for being inconsistent with the way you sow. Whatever you give out will come back to you; it's called *karma*, as the world calls it. But the Word says, you will reap what you sow – that's it. (See Galatians 6:7)

You may be saying, "I want a good relationship with my husband, but I have a hard time getting along with my husband." For example, a woman told me about her marriage counseling sessions and the reasons why adulterous things were happening. The crux of the matter was that she was mean before she got married, and was still mean afterwards. She eventually pushed her husband away because she didn't trust him. The husband said the reason he was creeping around was simply because he was raised by a single mother; and when tension arose, instead of creating more friction, he left and slept around. So he brought that behavioral pattern into his marriage.

You have to understand that your cup can overflow with the things God has anointed in your life. Your cup can either run over with good or bad. You are in control of what comes out of the cup based upon what you've allowed the Shepherd to do in your life. We have to watch what we place into our cups, because when things start to overflow, it comes in contact with other things. You put paper in the cup and when it overflows, any paper and equipment around it will get messed up. So any damaging thing that you put in that cup can affect anybody (relationships, friendships, etc.) around you when it finally overflows. When a cup of Kool-Aid spills over, it leaves a sticky residue that attracts ants and it stains wherever it lands. We have to make sure that our cups are filled with positive things.

Hurting people will hurt other people, but loving people will definitely bring love to others. It's just like perfume in that if I wear a well perfumed dress and go out to hug someone else, my perfume would rub off on that person, but if I'm funky and I go to hug someone, my funk is going to make that person stink as well. That is still an overflow. Some people only think of the overflow as a positive thing. Recall that what you sow is what you reap. It's a universal law that holds all the time.

What Is Overflowing from Your Cup?

Be aware that, in a matter of time, what you don't allow God to anoint and perfect in your life will show forth one way or the other. If you're bitter, your kids and the atmosphere around you will be bitter. The Bible tells us that when the righteous are in power, the people rejoice – they prosper. (See Proverbs 29:2) They rejoice because there is righteousness and love. But when the wicked rule, the people mourn – wickedness affects and infects. Therefore, is the cup overflowing in your life affecting you and others in a positive way or a negative way? When you get around people, do you always get the same positive results or the same negative results? If you see negative things overflowing from your cup, just go back and reevaluate its contents.

More so, you have to make sure no one is filling your cup with things that are toxic to you or to others, and that will make you become dysfunctional. So ask yourself, what has God anointed me to do? You know what you're anointed to do by what you do all the time and what people expect from you. You don't need a prophet to tell you that. If little children are always clinging to you…you're possibly anointed to work with kids. If teenagers are always asking you for advice…you're anointed to work with teenagers in some capacity. If people are always asking for strategic financial advice…that's the area where you should be of service to others. With regard to anything you have a knack or a passion for, God can anoint you to work with it for your benefit and that of others.

The next question to ask yourself is, "What is coming out of my cup? What is overflowing out of your cup?" The LORD has given you a word, saying, *"I will bless those who bless you and I will curse those who curse you."* (See Genesis 12:3) It means God is going to bless you for blessing me, and He's going to curse you for cursing me. We are all His children and we have right to the promise. You are just as special and precious to God as your neighbor. You have to make sure that wherever your cup is placed, it will have a positive effect on whomever is around when it overflows. If it's not so, you will have to turn to God immediately for deliverance. You don't have time to be short of any blessings coming from the Father, because you can't get your feelings and emotions in line.

Moreover, you have to make sure that you are allowing God to anoint every aspect of your life that He wills because it can affect not just you, but also both the present and the unborn generations. You have to allow God to fill your cups with good things if you don't want your children and your children's children to be cursed generation after generation – this is a great way to avoid what is called a generational curse. You have to nip it in the bud when you first realize that your cup is tainted by a bad thing. When you come in contact with tainted cups that taste sour or bitter, pause awhile to evaluate, empty and wash the cup, and then start over. Sometimes it is necessary to throw the cup away and allow God to give you a new one afresh. Whatever God considers the most appropriate way to deal with you, let Him have His way. His thoughts are always of good things as He desires to give you the expected end He has in view for your life. (See Jeremiah 29:11)

CHAPTER 6

The LORD
Saves & Keeps Me

"Surely goodness and mercy shall follow me all the days of my life: and I will dwell in the house of the LORD for ever." (Psalm 23:6)

Life can be hard sometimes, but we have to believe that things are going to get better. The Bible tells us that *"weeping may endure for a night, but joy cometh in the morning."* (Psalm 30:5).

As we prepare to close out this book in this last chapter, it is important to remember some keys from the previous chapters.

In verse one, we understand that we sign a contract that makes God our Shepherd, our LORD. We have to make sure that we self-examine what is overflowing from of our cups, either positive or negative. Our cups are going to be filled with whatever we allow. The song, *"Lord I'm Available to You,"* wherein a line says, "I've emptied out my cup, so that you can fill me up" is a perfect example of how to get our cups filled with and full of God.

In previous chapters, we also covered the scriptures concerning God restoring us, leading us on the path of righteousness, making us lie down in green pastures, leading us beside the still waters, taking us through the valley and shadow of death, helping us fear no evil, comforting us with His rod and His staff after they have been applied, anointing us for what He wants us to do, giving us the purpose to live for, making our cup run over with whatever is in us, and then bringing us to a place of divine certainty of His goodness as we come to 'surely.' All of the things that happen before the Almighty God guarantees us that goodness and mercy are going to follow us.

Goodness and Mercy

Psalm 23:6 says, *"Surely goodness and mercy shall follow me all the days of my life."* The word *goodness* could mean positive, blessings, beauty, and safety. The word *mercy* could mean grace, protection, and forgiveness. The word surely means it's a definite, guaranteed and assured thing that will happen. God has been revealing to me how every scripture, line upon line, and precept upon precept, is building up to a finer conclusion that we should be able to dwell in the house of the LORD forever. That's the final conclusion! His presence is the key to that benevolence He longs to manifest toward us.

But what does goodness really mean? A lot of people sum it up as favor, but when I looked up the word, goodness, I found out it really deals with being aggressive. So basically, it's an aggressive virtue that will continue to be with you in a positive way. However, discipline comes with that virtue being with you. As much as the blessings are going to come for the rest of your lives, God is also going to be "whopping our butts" for the rest of our lives just keep us in line, because He loves us. He never wants us to get comfortable doing the same thing or going in the direction He hasn't ordained. For example, your parents do not care how old you get, they will always tell you when they think you're doing right or wrong.

More often, we get very excited about the blessings and mercy following us, which we should, but we hardly take discipline into consideration. We are going to be disciplined by God that we may do better as required of us, because His name is on that contract with us. Consequently, He is constantly trying to make sure we are checked for greatness. It's time to grow up, but in growing up, discipline has to constantly be in force. If not, we will squander the grace and opportunities He has provided for our good. He gives us all things to enjoy, but then He wants to direct us on how to utilize His provisions. Then mercy steps into play.

What does mercy actually mean? It is God withholding punishments that we rightfully deserve. Let me expatiate how goodness and mercy coincide with each other. Let's go back to the previous example on parental discipline. When kids mess up, sometimes, their parents may choose not to whoop them because of the tremendous love they have for their children. In the same way, if God punished us for every wrong thing we did, we would be in trouble for the rest of our lives. The Bible says, *"All have sinned and come short of the glory of God..."* (See Romans 3:23-24). If we focus solely on the goodness part of the verse, His blessings are there, His understanding is there, but we do not usually put into consideration the forgiveness or unconditional love that comes along with that mercy.

When I read about God's forgiveness, the Scripture teaches us that His mercies are new every morning. So, when God has forgiven you of something, He's not holding it against you. Don't let the sun go down on your anger. That lets us know that when God puts an issue to rest, He lays it to rest in the sea of forgetfulness. That's a good God. It's really astonishing that God gets up with a mindset, *"She may mess up today, but I'm still going to treat her well; and just in case she messes up, I'm going to be there to extend my unlimited mercy."*

> *Arise, and go down to the potter's house, and there I will cause thee to hear my words. Then I went down to the potter's house, and, behold, he wrought a work on the wheels.* (Jeremiah 18:2-3)

In all probability, God loves to extend grace when we are in situations where our flesh can't handle the pressure of life; His peace will flow so that our character isn't questioned, because He fully understands that life is trying to get us down. God understands our nature as human beings, and He understands that in our efforts to do good, we may go wrong. He understands that because we've made Him LORD, we have allowed Him to come in and set us on the Potter's wheel where He has the tool required to pull out all of our imperfections. God loves it when He sees progress, when growth is happening in our lives. As a result, God makes sure we are protected along the way as we are growing.

Keep Moving

At no point in time do we see God cause us to stop moving in life, until it is time to rest. During the trials of the valley of the shadow of death, we wouldn't even stop, but keep going in the direction He points us to. Through everyday life, when you are making our mistakes, you have to keep going without looking back. What you have to realize from Psalm 23 is that when life gets hard, we cannot stop. One thing that irks me about some Christians is when they stop on God because they feel that their problem has been going on too long to get solved. They get "pissed off" about everything and at everyone. It irks me when some Christians focus more on the situation, instead of God in the situation. Well, it may surprise you to know that the situation may not change, but God is always in the situation.

Generally speaking, Psalm 23 is trying to teach us that we should change our perspective, our mentality, our orientation about God and life generally. Storms are not going to stop - you won't stop passing through tough times. Every year, Florida expects a hurricane, and they get it. However, the real Floridians get prepared for the hurricanes because they know the storms are coming. You're either approaching it or leaving the storm. The good thing to note is that some storms are used as cleansing mechanisms. God doesn't always use them as punishments. Sometimes, we need to be broken, and then become rebuilt because we weren't built on a firm foundation.

Furthermore, when David was writing Psalm 23, he was trying to teach us how to build our faith in God and how to weather the storm. He was teaching us that while we are going through the storm, we have to keep moving forward to fulfill the purpose of God in our lives. God has anointed us to for a given purpose, but if we don't go through His building process, we are holding up the goodness of God, which has been placed upon our lives. We have to understand that the word good is a powerful word.

If we look back in Genesis, after everything God created, He said it was "good." He didn't say it was excellent, awesome, magnificent, or the bomb; He said it was good. So, why do we always try to diminish and underestimate the power of *good* in the way we use it today?

Good, according to the Almighty God, was the best term to use when He talked about His creation. When He looked at man, He said, "That's good." When He looked at the sun and the stars, He said, "That's good." So, for His goodness to follow us means His best is following us. If His best is following us, what we need to do is bring our mindset to a place where we can physically say, "Whatever God has in store for me is good, but I'm also prepared for His correction."

God Will Keep You

How does the statement, *"surely goodness and mercy shall follow me all the days of my life"* connect with *"and I will dwell in the house of the LORD forever?"* The synergy thereof protects your salvation; and in the end, your soul will be saved. It is the goodness and the mercy of God following you all the days of your life that will help keep your soul preserved from destruction so that you can spend eternity in heaven with God. (See I Peter 1:3-5)

You have to understand that it is God's correction, mercy, and blessings along life's journey that can keep you till the end so you can spend eternity with God. If you live in the anointing, it will keep you safe; and in the end, you can reign in heaven with Him. Living in the anointing connects you to the scripture that says, *"to live is Christ, and to die is gain,"* (Philippians 1:21). To suffer with Him, and to rule and reign, that is the key to getting into heaven. It's just that easy. We must allow God's correction to work in our lives so that in the end our souls will be saved. We also have to allow God's goodness to follow us for the rest of our lives so that we'll have reasons to be joyful in the midst of sorrow and affliction.

We have to understand what's waiting for us when we spend our eternity with Him. The Bible says, *"In my father's house are many mansions."* (John 14:2). It's not just about going to heaven, but understanding that I have benefits because Psalm 23:1-6 has been applied to my situation, and it's in effect in my life. I'm going to get my crown, drink my milk and honey, wear my long white robe, and everything else that is in store for me because I have made the LORD my Shepherd, and I have allowed Him to lead me all the days of my life.

ABOUT THE AUTHOR

Pastor Chrislyn M. Davis-Haynes was born on February 23, 1980 in Atlanta, Georgia and is married to Deacon Chevaughn Michael Haynes. She is the mother of a beautiful, little girl named Caroline Michelle Haynes. The youngest and only daughter of three children born to the late Deacon Michael Davis and Pastor Carol Rawls Davis, Chrislyn (a.k.a. Markell) graduated from Southwest DeKalb High School with an Advanced Academic Diploma. Having a desire to receive every level of degree offered, Pastor Davis-Haynes holds an Associate in Teacher Education, Bachelor of Arts in Early Childhood Education, Masters in Christian School Administration, and a Specialist Degree in Leadership and Supervision. In addition, she is a certified Clown, a certified Personal Trainer, and Caterer (Made with Love Catering).

Pastor Davis-Haynes accepted Jesus Christ into her life at a very young age. While asleep one night, at the age of 12, she was visited in a dream. The Lord showed her a vision and the focus was centered on a phrase He wrote across the sky, "the gospel will surely come again." Not understanding completely, but totally overwhelmed, she shared the vision with her mother. Pastor Carol Davis interpreted the vision and encouraged her to hold it close to her heart. Since 1995, she has been determined to live for God and God alone.

Pastor Davis-Haynes has been a member of Anointed Word Christian Ministries International since its founding in 1995, under the leadership of the late Pastor and Founder Carol Rawls Davis. Pastor Davis-Haynes is actively involved with and serves as the workout instructor for the TIP Health Ministry. Continuing the legacy in Education started by her mother, she serves as the Administrator and Principal of Anointed Word Christian School International and Miracle Early Learning Center, which are entities of Anointed Word Christian Ministries International, Incorporated.

Since taking the helm of the ministry in August 2011, Pastor Davis-Haynes has continued the legacy left by her mother; to develop mature Christians by teaching the Word of God without compromise. Her goal is to present God in such a way that people will develop a relationship and fall in love with Him for themselves. Along with her brother, Bishop Mark Maxey Davis and Chief Elder Chris Davis and with the support of her husband Deacon Chevaughn, who works alongside her in the ministry, the results of her teaching are becoming an eye-seeing reality. The base scriptures for her life and ministry are Romans 5:3-5 and Luke 9:1-6. Pastor Chrislyn Markell Davis-Haynes is a fun and energetic woman who is madly in love with God and wants to please Him in every aspect of her life.

CONTACT INFORMATION

AUTHOR

Pastor Chrislyn Markell Davis- Haynes
404.317.2706
404.241.8200
cmdavisawcsi@bellsouth.net
www.cmdavishaynes.com

PUBLISHER

MEWE, LLC
404.482.3135
mewecorporation@gmail.com
www.mewellc.com

www.ingramcontent.com/pod-product-compliance
Lightning Source LLC
LaVergne TN
LVHW021540080426
835509LV00019B/2756